Primary School
Mathematics Dictionary
Key Concepts

First published in 2019 by Succeedu Education Ltd

Copyright © 2019 by Steven Rhodes

All rights reserved. No part of this publication may be reproduced, distributed, or transmitted in any form or by any means, including photocopying, recording, or other electronic or mechanical methods, without the prior written permission of the publisher.

ISBN: 978-1-9160220-0-3

SUCCEEDU is a registered trademark of Succeedu Education Ltd.

Succeedu Education Ltd
Kemp House
160 City Road
London
EC1V 2NX
United Kingdom
0203 34880846
info@succeedu.co.uk

www.succeedu-books.com
www.succeedu.co.uk

Cover design
Zest Creative Co., ltd
www.zest-creative.com

For Ian, Nitesh and
the team at Zest Creative.
Thank you.

Introduction

The Primary Mathematics dictionary by Succeedu Education uses simple language and illustrations to define the key concepts in the subject.

This dictionary is designed for children, parents and teachers to use as a reference so that everybody involved in the learning process is reading from the same page. Supporting young children in developing the ability to independently think, act and search for understanding is a key skill in our rapidly changing world.

This book is written for:

Children: Definitions are simple and easy-to-understand. The pictures and illustrations help young learners consolidate and deepen their learning from the classroom.

Parents: Helping with homework can be a challenge at times and not knowing the current language or processes used in today's primary schools can be frustrating. Use the dictionary as a tool to keep up-to-date with your child's learning.

Teachers: Use the dictionary as a reference for lesson planning or to refresh your understanding.

I hope you find this book useful

Steven

A-Z Mathematics Dictionary

abstract number: A number used without referring to anything e.g. 4, 8, 20. A number that does refer to something is said to be concrete e.g. 4 bottles, 8 footballs.

acute angle: An angle that is less than 90⁰.

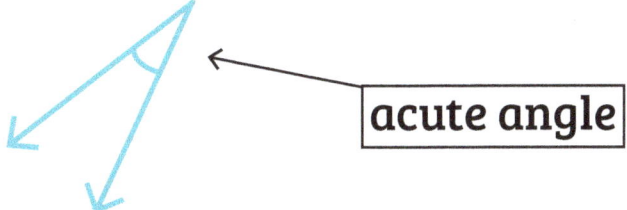

add/addition: An operation that combines two or more numbers. The symbol for addition is +.

addend: The name of each number in an addition calculation.

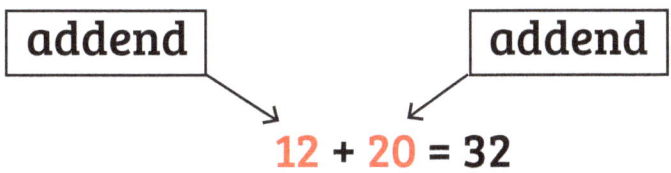

algebra: The part of mathematics in which letters and symbols are used instead of numbers. We use letters when we don't know the actual values of the numbers. We use letters and numbers to write equations.

$$a + 8 = 10$$

A-Z Mathematics Dictionary

algorithm: A process or set of rules in calculations or other problem-solving operations. Algorithms are often used in computer programs.

angle: A measurement of turn measured in degrees (°). There are 360° in a full turn.

anti-clockwise: The opposite direction to the way the hands of a clock move.

anti-clockwise

area: The amount of space inside a flat 2D shape.

area of a rectangle

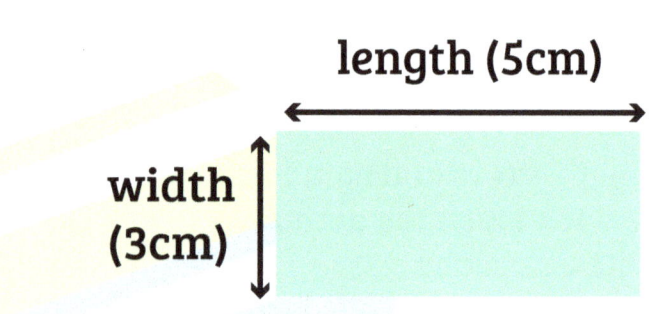

Formula
area = length (l) x width (w)
area = l x w
area = 5 cm x 3 cm
area = $25cm^2$

A-Z Mathematics Dictionary

arithmetic: An area of mathematics that deals with numbers. Mostly addition, subtraction, multiplication and division.

array: An arrangement of objects, pictures or numbers in columns and rows is called an array.

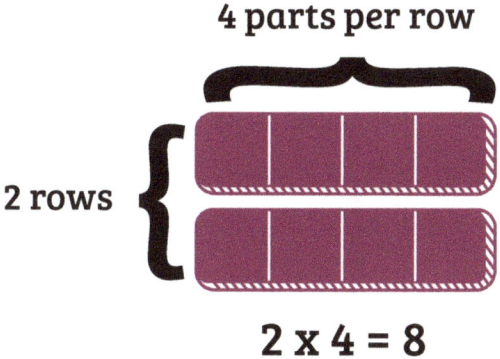

ascending order: Numbers or objects arranged in order from smallest to largest. (See also descending order.)

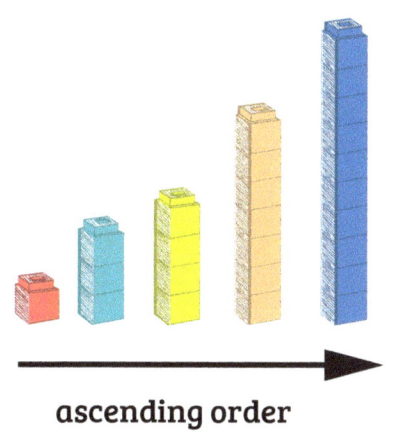

2, 5, 7, 14, 24, 56

ascending order

A-Z Mathematics Dictionary

average: A number used represent the central or typical value in a set of data. (See also mean, median and mode.)

axis(i): (Plural axes) Lines that are used to locate points on a graph. The vertical line is called the y-axis and the horizontal line is called th x-axis.

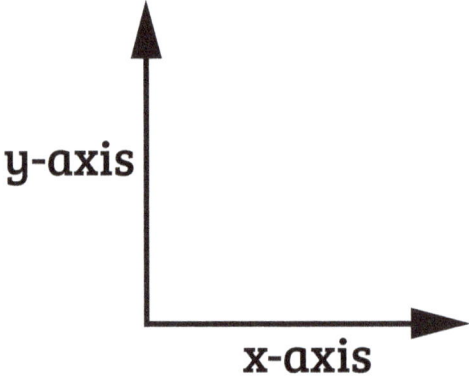

axis(ii): (Plural axes) The imaginary line about which a body rotates. e.g. The Earth rotates on an axis.

A-Z Mathematics Dictionary

Babylonian number system: A number system used by the ancient Babylonian civilisation.

1. 𒐕	6. 𒐚	11. 𒌋𒐕	16. 𒌋𒌋𒌋
2. 𒐖	7. 𒐛	12. 𒌋𒐖	17. 𒌋𒌋𒌋𒐕
3. 𒐗	8. 𒐜	13. 𒌋𒌋	18. 𒌋𒌋𒌋𒐖
4. 𒐘	9. 𒐝	14. 𒌋𒌋𒐕	19. 𒌋𒌋𒌋𒐗
5. 𒐙	10. 𒌋	15. 𒌋𒌋𒐖	20. 𒌋𒌋𒌋𒌋

bar graph: A graph that uses rectangular bars to show different values of data.

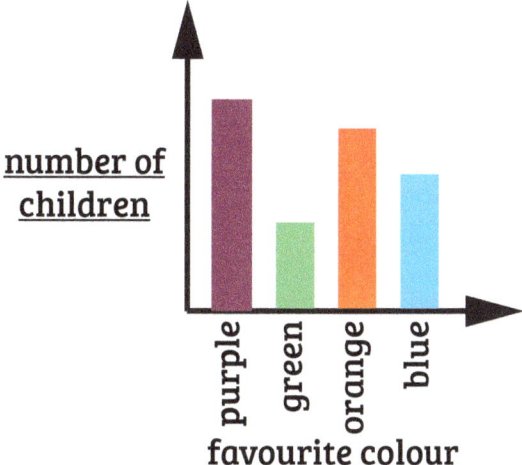

bar line graph: A graph that uses lines to show different values of data in the same way as a bar chart.

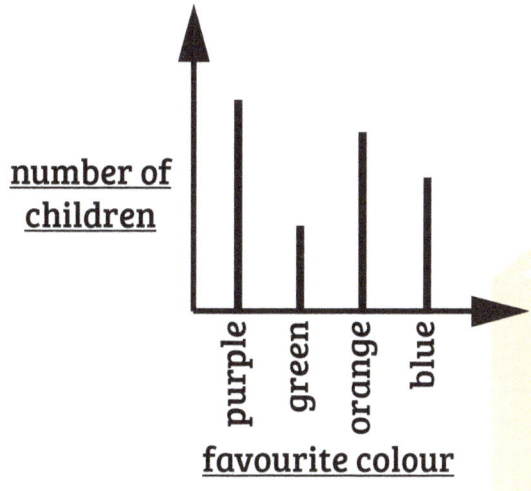

A-Z Mathematics Dictionary

bisect: To divide a line or shape into two equal parts.

BODMAS: The order of operations when solving a calculation.

Brackets   ( ) [ ] { }
Order power of   √ ( )²
Division   / ÷
Multiplication   * x
Addition   +
Subtraction   —

Example: 10 + (3 x 2) =
Using BODMAS, brackets first
1. (3 x 2) = 6
2. 10 + 6 = 16

calculate: To use the operations of addition, subtraction, multiplication and division to solve a problem.

capacity: The total amount of liquid a container can hold.

This container has a capacity of 1 litre.

A-Z Mathematics Dictionary

carroll diagram: A four square diagram used to sort objects based on two different characteristics.

	At least one line of symmetry	No line of symmetry
Quadrilateral	■	▰
Non Quadrilateral	⬡	▲

chunking: A method for dividing. Instead of sharing or grouping, this method uses chunks of a number and calculates how many of these chunks can divide into the dividend. In simple terms how many times will one number fit into another number. It can be done in a column and on a number line.

$27 \div 3 = 9$

```
  27
- 15   (5 x 3)
  12
  12   (4 x 3)
   0
```

$27 \div 3 = 9$

+15 (5 x 3), +6 (2 x 3), +6 (2 x 3)

0 — 15 — 21 — 27

A-Z Mathematics Dictionary

circumference: The distance around the outside of a circle.

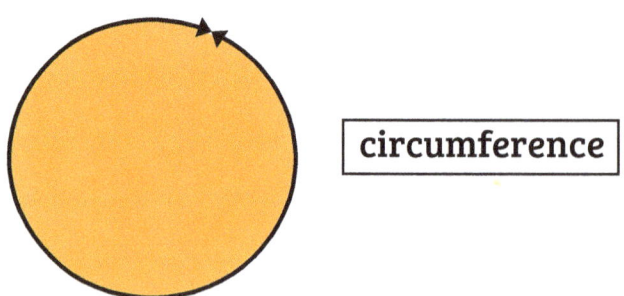

classify: To group things according to a category.

Four legs   Two legs

clockwise: To move in the same direction as the hands of a clock.

clockwise

A-Z Mathematics Dictionary

column: Numbers or objects arranged vertically.

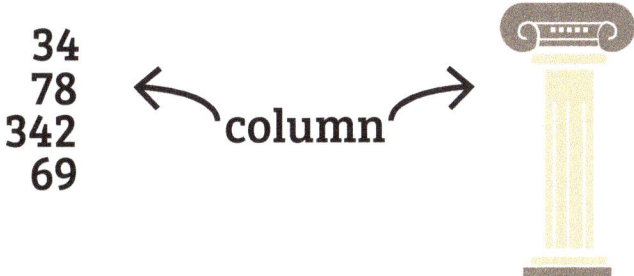

common denominator: When two or more fractions have the same denominator.

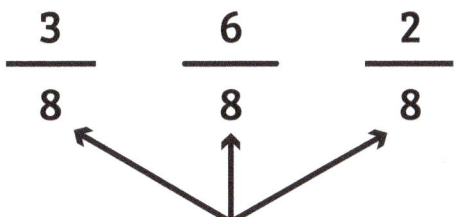

common denominator

common difference: The difference between two numbers in a number sequence. The difference between consecutive numbers is the same.

A-Z Mathematics Dictionary

common factor: A number that is a factor of two or more numbers. (See also factor.)

Factors of 16: **1 2 4** 8 16

Factors of 20: **1 2 4** 5 10 20

Common Factors of 16 and 20: **1** , **2** , **4**

compare: To compare two numbers we usually use subtraction or division.

<u>Compare numbers 5 and 15</u>

15 is 10 more than 5 ⟶ 15 - 5 = 10 (subtraction)

15 is 3 times more than 5 ⟶ 15 ÷ 5 = 3 (division)

compass points: Used to show direction. The directions can be remembered using different mnemonics.

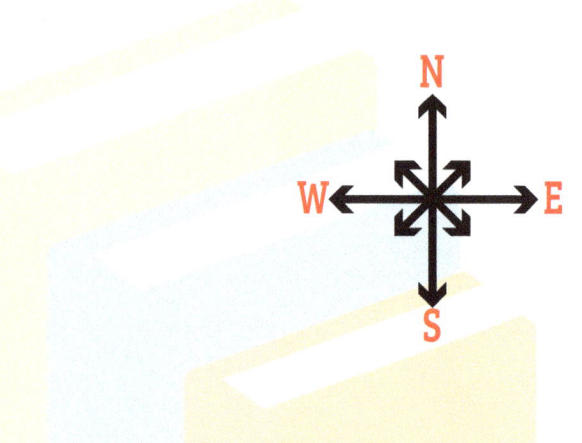

Naughty **E**lephants **S**quirt **W**ater

Never **E**at **S**quiggly **W**orms

Never **E**at **S**hredded **W**heat

A-Z Mathematics Dictionary

composite number: A number than can be divided by more than 1 and itself. It has more than 2 factors. (See also prime number.)

<u>Factors of 10</u>:   1 , 2 , 5 , 10 - composite number
<u>Factors of 7</u>:   1 , 7 - prime number

compound number: An amount shown using more than one unit of measurment.

4 metres 36 centimetres

concentric: Circles that are inside each other and have the same centre.

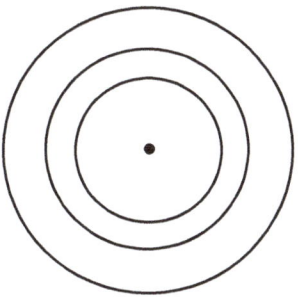

concrete number: (see also abstract number). A number that refers to specific objects

4 bottles of milk
6 bananas

cone: A 3D shape with a circular base, a curved, smooth surface and a point at the top.

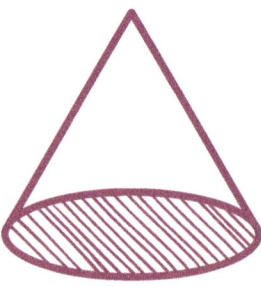

congruent: Shapes that are the exact same size as each other no matter what their position.

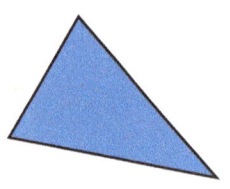  

consecutive: Numbers or events that follow after each other.

consecutive numbers: 5 , 6 , 7 , 8 , 9

consecutive months: March , April , May , June , July

A-Z Mathematics Dictionary

continuous data: Data that can be measured at any point and has an infinite number of possible values. (See also discrete data.)

continuous data: height, rainfall, temperature

discrete data: favourite colour, cars, sports

co-ordinates: A pair of values that show the exact position on a graph or map.

co-ordinates point A: (3,4)

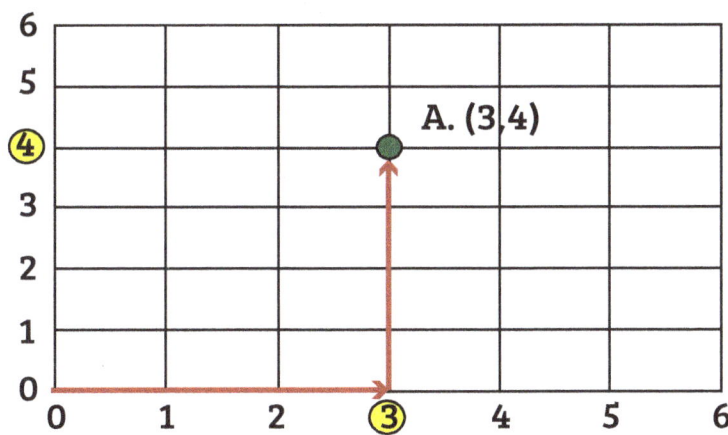

cube: A 3D shape with 6 square faces that are all the same size.

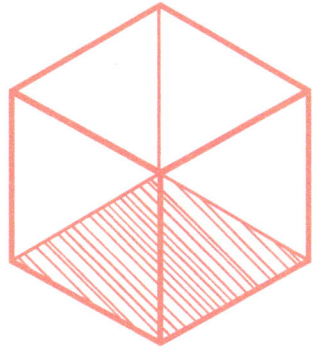

cuboid: A 3D shape with either 6 rectangular faces or 4 rectangular faces and 2 square faces.

cylinder: A 3D shape with 2 circular faces and 1 curved surface joining to the edges of the circular faces.

data: Information, facts or numbers collected, and often shown in tables and graphs.

decimal number: A number with a decimal point in it.

5.36

A-Z Mathematics Dictionary

decimal place: The place a digit sits in relation to the decimal point.

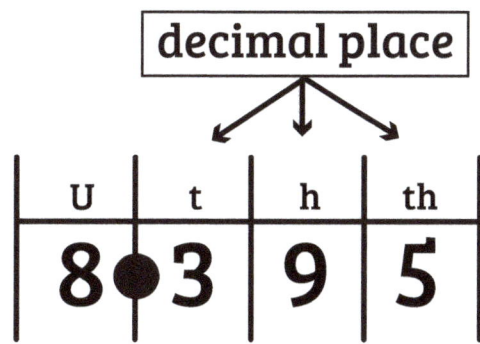

decimal point: A point that separates whole numbers from digits that are less than 1 whole number.

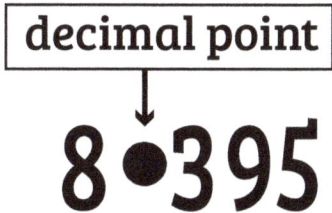

degree(i): A unit of measurment for the amount of turn in an angle. The symbol for degree °

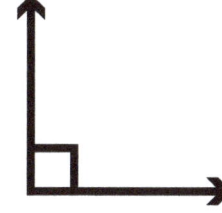

The angle is 90 degrees, 90°

degree(ii): A unit of measurement for temperature.

Degree Celcius   °C
Degree Fahrenheit   °F

denominator: The bottom digit of a fraction.

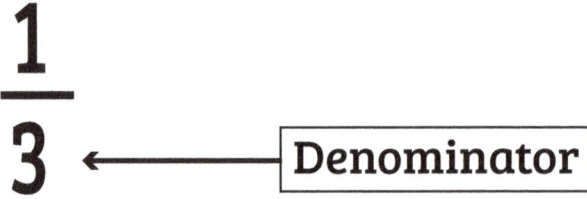

descending order: Numbers or objects arranged in order from largest to smallest. (See ascending order.)

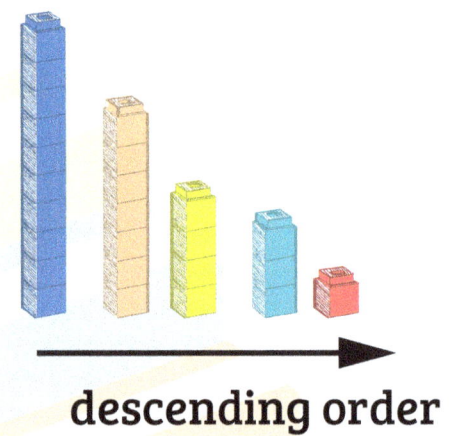

56, 24, 14, 7, 5, 2
descending order

A-Z Mathematics Dictionary

diagonal: In a 2D shape, a diagonal line is a straight line joining two vertices that are not adjacent (i.e. not next door). In a 3D shape a diagonal line line is a straight line joining opposite vertices

diameter: A straight line that passes from the edge of a circle, through the centre and to the edge of the circle on the opposite side.

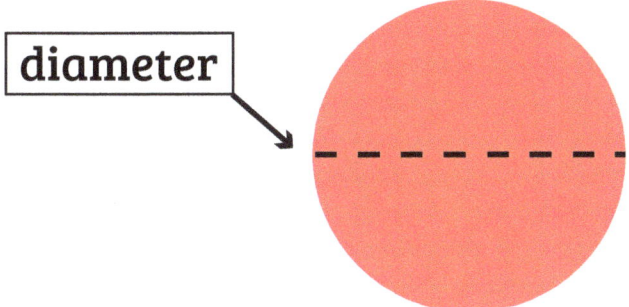

difference: How much one number is more or less than another number. Difference is calculated by subtraction.

The difference between 11 and 5 is 6

11 - 5 = 6

A-Z Mathematics Dictionary

digit: Any of the numbers from 0 to 9. The digits are 0, 1, 2, 3, 4, 5, 7, 8, 9. Many numbers have more than one digit.

375 has three digits **3**, **7** and **5**

discrete data: Data that can be counted and placed into a group. e.g. favourite colour or favourite sport. (See continuous data.)

dividend: The number that is being divided in a division calculation.

dividend → **20** ÷ 4 = 5

divisible (by): If a number (a) is divided equally by number (b), we say that (a) is divisible by (b).

$$15 \div 5 = 3$$
$$15 \div 3 = 5$$

15 is divisible by 3 & 5

A-Z Mathematics Dictionary

division: This is the inverse (opposite) of multiplication. Division can be seen as sharing or grouping.

Sharing

$6 \div 2$

6 counters are shared between 2 people. How many counters does each person get?

Grouping

$6 \div 2$

There are 6 counters. How many people can have 2 counters each?

divisor: The number that does the dividing.

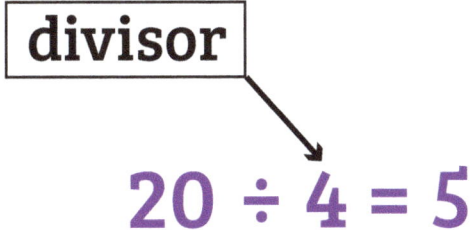

$$20 \div 4 = 5$$

dodecahedron: A 12 sided 3D shape.

A regular dodecahedron is made from 12 regular pentagons.

edge: The line where two faces meet in a 3D shape.

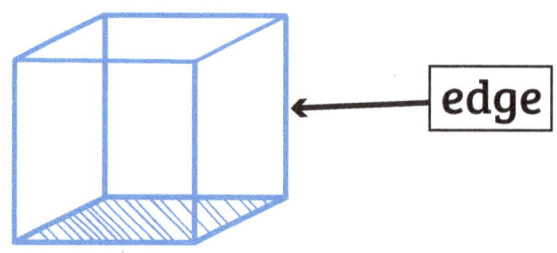

Egyptian number system: A number system used by the Ancient Egyptians.

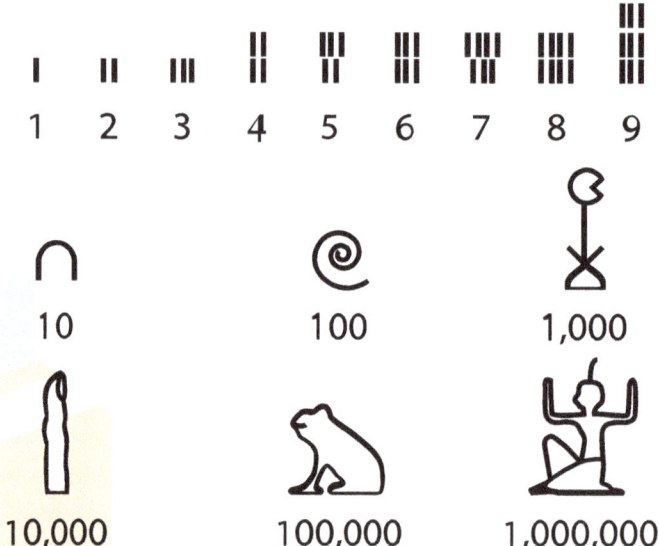

A-Z Mathematics Dictionary

equal: When two or more things have the same value.

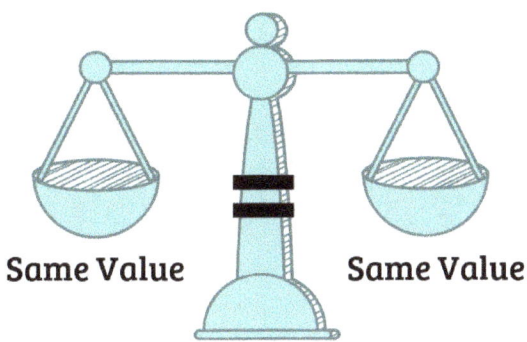

equal chance: When the chance of one event happening is the same as the chance of another event happening.

Heads

Tails

equilateral triangle: A triangle where all three sides are equal lengths and all three internal angles are equal (60°).

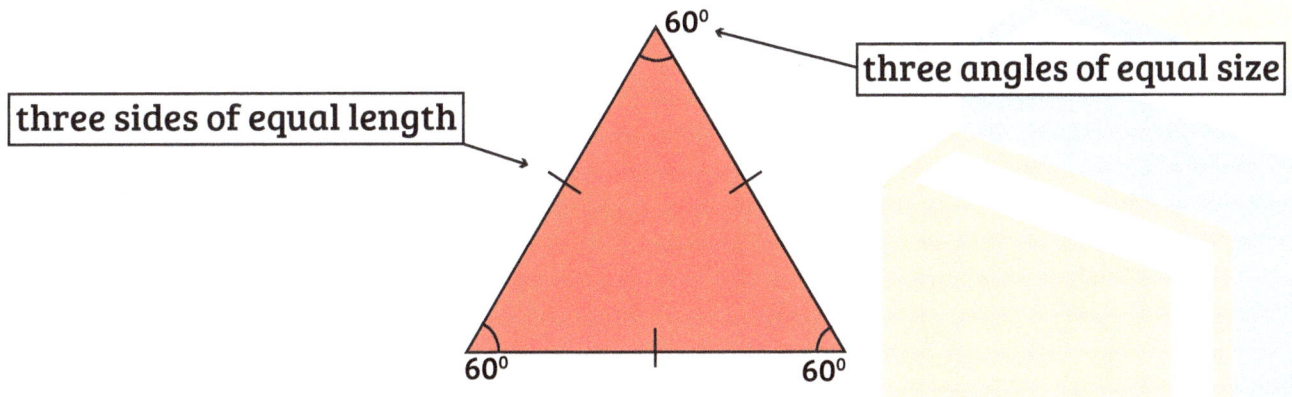

equivalent: When two or more things have the same value or same amount.

equivalent fractions: When two or more fractions have a different numerator and denominator, but have the same value.

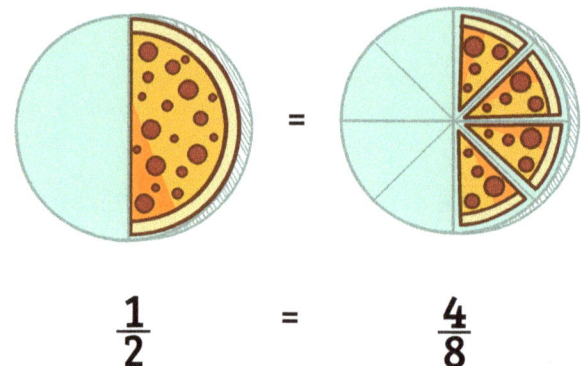

$$\frac{1}{2} = \frac{4}{8}$$

estimate: To use information that you have already, to make an educated guess.

I know the length of a metre stick, so I can estimate the length of a swimming pool.

A-Z Mathematics Dictionary

even: A number that is divisible by 2.

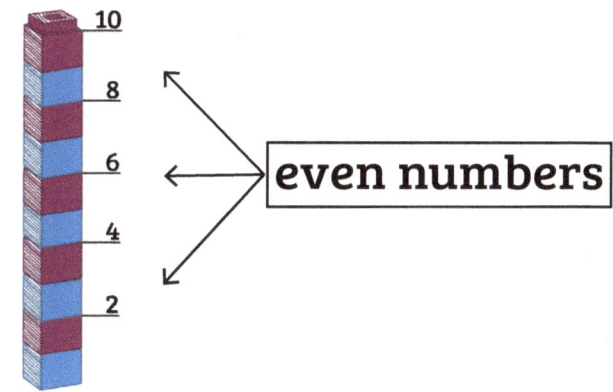

even chance: (See equal chance.)

exchange: When moving an amount from one place value to another place value, it is called an exchange. E.g. exchange ten 1s for one 10.

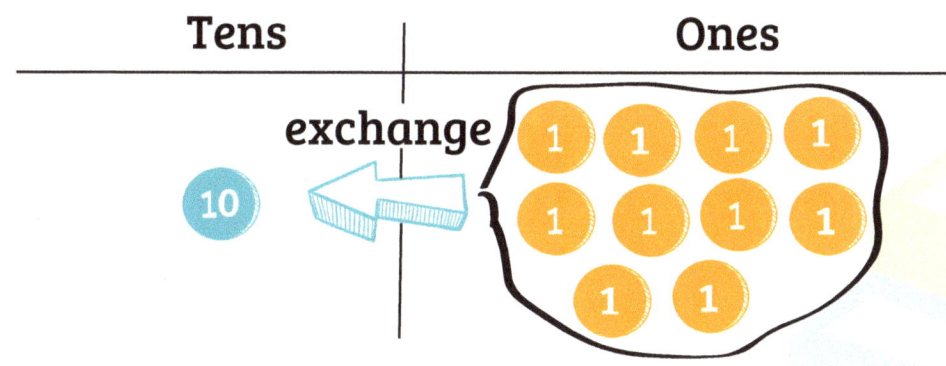

F

A-Z Mathematics Dictionary

face: The flat surface of a 3D shape.

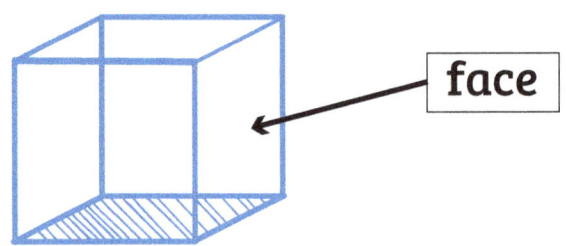

factor: A factor is a number that will divide equally into another number.

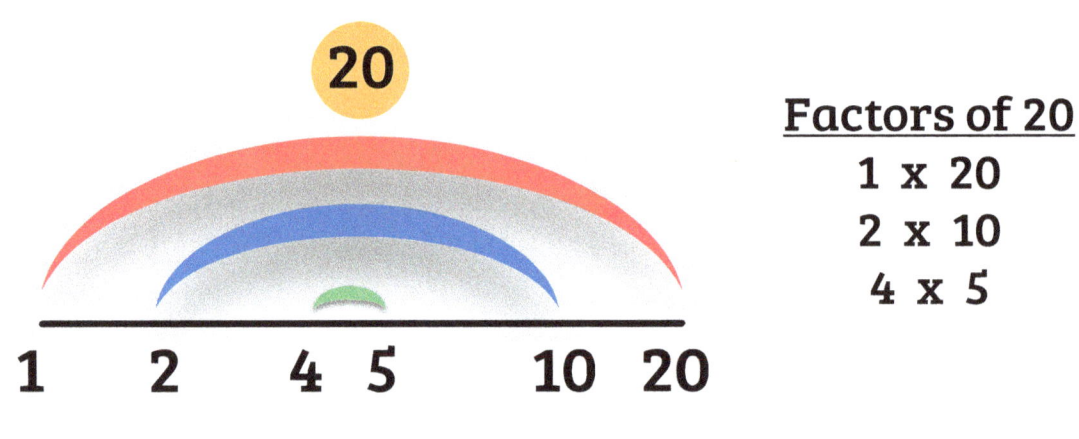

Factors of 20 = 1,2,4,5,10 and 20

A-Z Mathematics Dictionary

fraction: An amount or value that is less than a whole number. The denominator is the number of equal parts the whole has been split into.

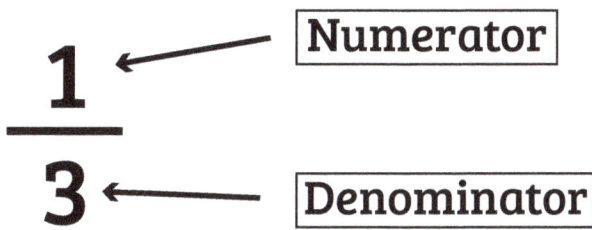

frequency table: A table that shows how often something occurs (frequency) of data. The frequency is often recorded as a tally.

Transport	Tally	Total
Car	⦀⦀ ⦀⦀ |	11
Bus	⦀⦀ ||	7
Train	|	3

A-Z Mathematics Dictionary

graph: A mathematical diagram that shows the relationship between two variables of data.   e.g. variable 1: number of children, varaiable 2: favourite colour.

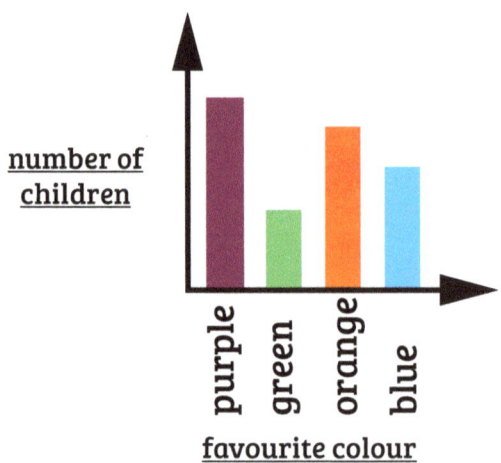

greater than: A symbol that is used to compare two quantities. It is used when the first quantity is larger than the second quality.

$$8 > 2$$
greater than

greater than or equal to: A symbol that is used to compare two quantities that are either great or equal to the second quantity.

$$8 \geq 2 \qquad 2 \geq 2$$
greater than or equal to   greater than or equal to

A-Z Mathematics Dictionary

grid multiplication: A method of multiplication that partitions numbers and places them in a grid. The partitioned digits of the first number are multiplied with the partitioned digits of the second number. Finally, they are added together.

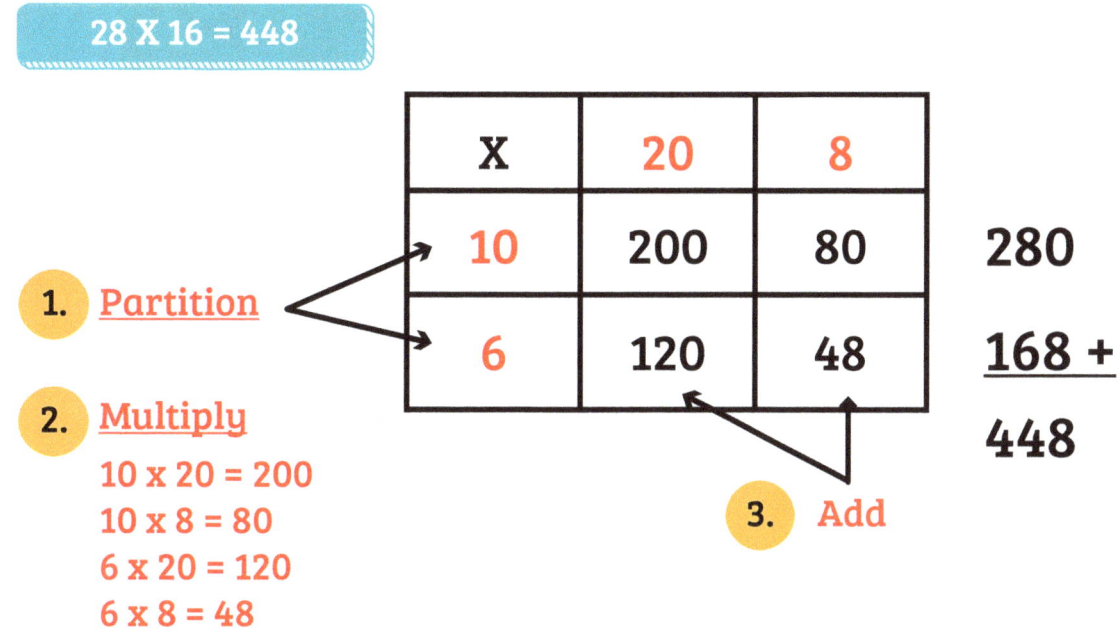

28 X 16 = 448

1. Partition

2. Multiply
   10 x 20 = 200
   10 x 8 = 80
   6 x 20 = 120
   6 x 8 = 48

3. Add

X	20	8
10	200	80
6	120	48

280
168 +
448

hemisphere: Half a sphere.

heptagon: A 2D shape with seven sides.

hexagon: A 2D shape with six sides.

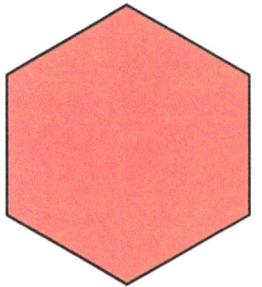

highest common factor: A common factor is a factor of two different numbers. The highest common factor is the largest of the common factors.

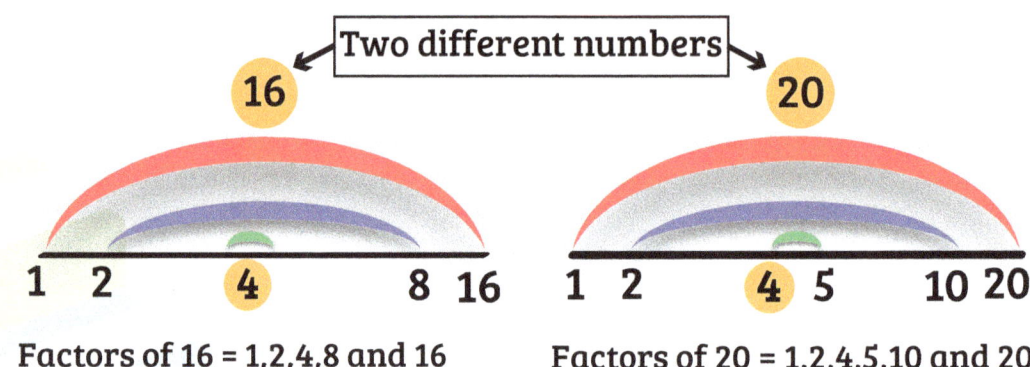

Factors of 16 = 1,2,4,8 and 16   Factors of 20 = 1,2,4,5,10 and 20

Common Factors of 16 and 20 = 1, 2 and 4

Highest Common Factor of 16 and 20 = 4

A-Z Mathematics Dictionary

horizontal: Something that lies flat to the horizon.

hypotenuse: The longest side of a rightangled triangle. It is the side that is opposite the right angle.

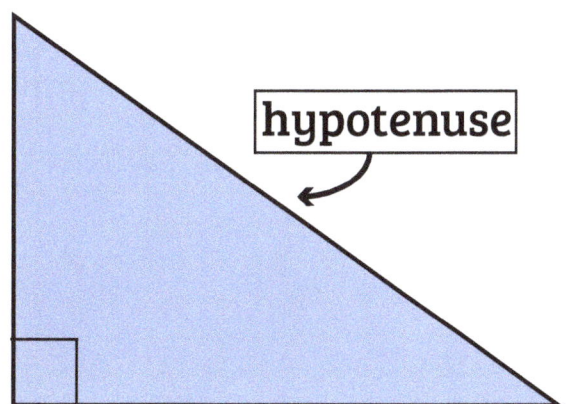

imperial system: A system of weights and measures originally developed in England.

Measure	Unit
Mass	16 ounces (oz) = 1 pound (lb)
	14 pounds = 1 stone
	8 stone = 1 hundredweight (cwt)
Length	12 inches (in) = 1 foot (ft)
	3 feet = 1 yard (yd)
	1760 yards = 1 mile
Area	144 square inches (sq. in.) = 1 square foot (sq. ft.)
	9 square feet = 1 square yard (sq. yd.)
	4840 square yards = 1 acre (A)
Volume	1728 cubic inches (cu. in.) = 1 cubic foot (cu. ft.)
	27 cubic feet = 1 cubic yard (cu.yd.)
Capacity	4 gills (gi) = 1 pint (pt)
	2 pints = 1 quart (qt)
	4 quarts (8 pints) = 1 gallon

A-Z Mathematics Dictionary

improper fraction: A type of fraction when the numerator is larger than the denominator.

$$\text{Numerator} \longrightarrow \frac{11}{8} \longleftarrow \text{Denominator}$$

integer: A number that is a whole number and not a fraction.

i) Positive integer is a number that is bigger than zero:

$$1, 2, 3, 4, 5$$

ii) Negative integer is a number that is less than zero:

$$-1, -2, -3, -4, -5$$

interior angle: The angles on the inside (interior) of a shape.

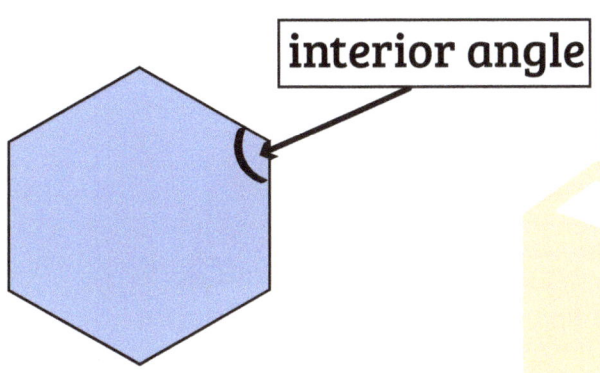

A-Z Mathematics Dictionary

inverse: Inverse operations are opposite operations. Addition is the opposite of subtraction; multiplication is the opposite of division; square root is the opposite of square numbers.

Inverse
325 + 15 = 340
340 - 15 = 325

irregular: An irregular polygon is one that has differnt length sides and different size angles.

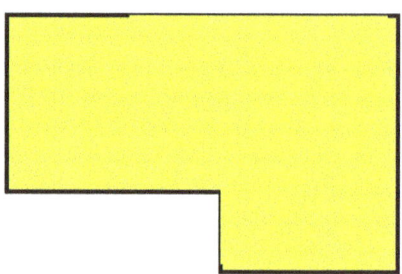

isosceles triangle: A triangle which has 2 sides of equal length and 2 angles of equal size. It also has 1 line of symmetry.

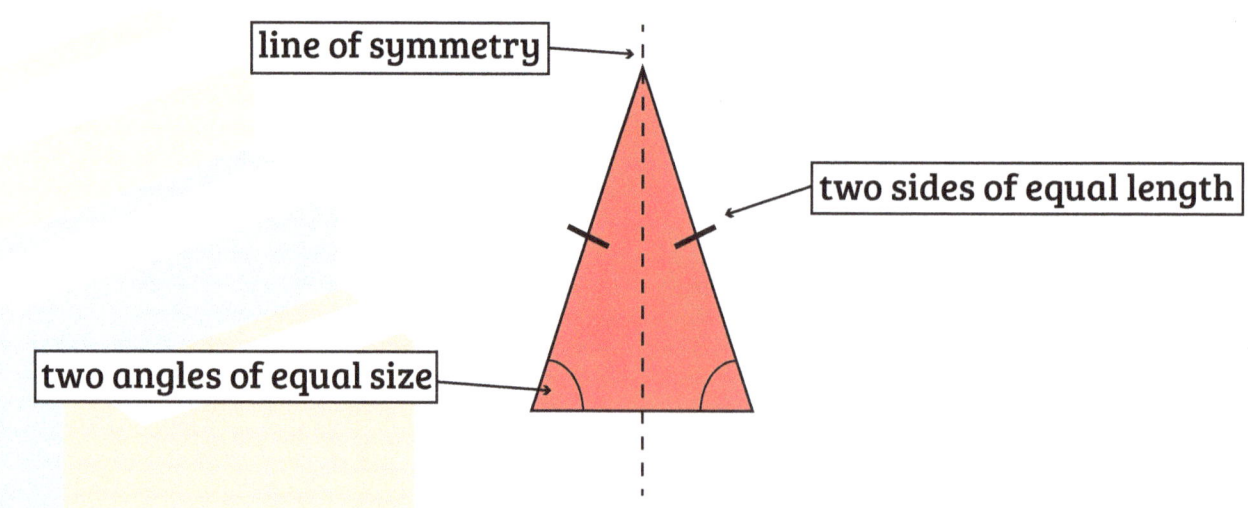

A-Z Mathematics Dictionary

kite: A kite is a quadrilateral (4 sided polygon). It has two sets of adjacent sides (next to each other) that are the same length. It has at least 1 line of symmetry. A rhombus and a square can also be called a kite.

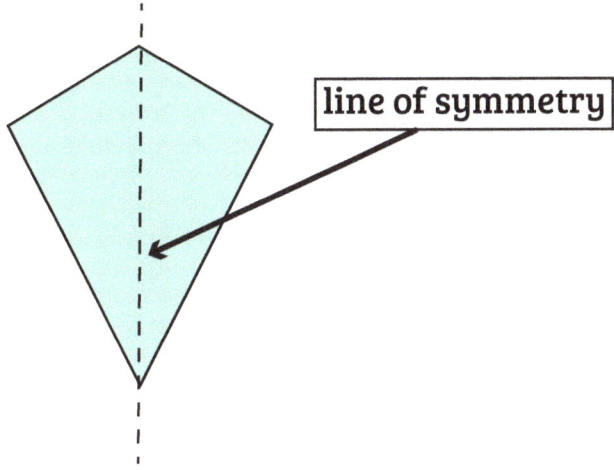

less than: A symbol that is used to compare two quantities. It is used when the first quantity is smaller than the second quantity.

$$2 < 8$$

less than

less than or equal to: A symbol that is used to compare two quantities that are either less than or equal to the second quantity.

$$2 \leq 8 \qquad 2 \leq 2$$

less than or equal to   less than or equal to

A-Z Mathematics Dictionary

line graph: A graph that shows continuous data. The data, such as amount of rainfall or temperature can be shown on a line graph.

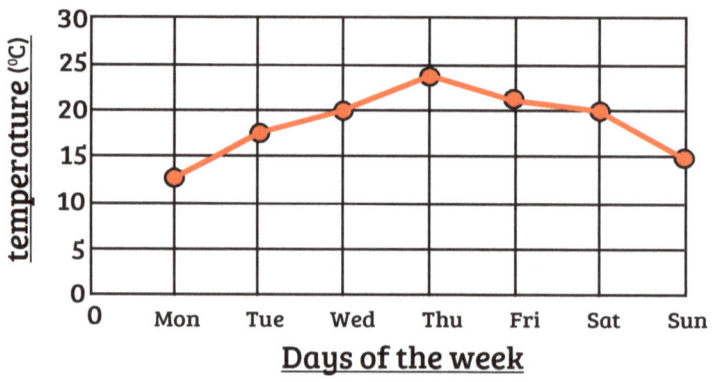

line of symmetry: A line through a shape so that when the shape is folded in half, along the line of symmetry, then the two halves match up.

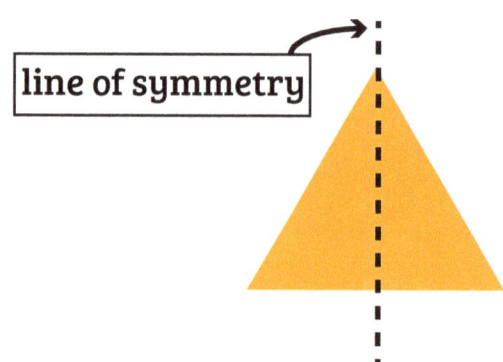

lowest common multiple: The lowest digit that is a multiple of two separate numbers. (See also multiple.)

Multiples of 2:   2   4   6   8   10   12   14   16   18

Multiples of 3:   3   6   9   12   15   18

Lowest Common Multiple of 2 and 3 is   6

A-Z Mathematics Dictionary

magic number: A square made up of smaller squares, with a number in each of the smaller squares. When each row, column or diagonal set of numbers are added, they always add up to the same value.

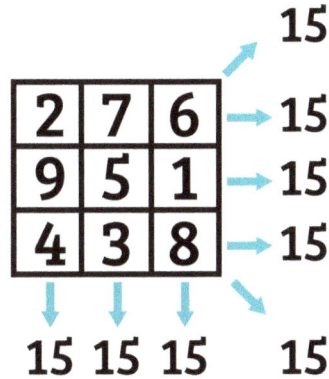

mass: The amount of matter contained within an object. Mass is usually measured using the metric system of milligrams (mg), grams (g), kilograms (kg) and tonnes (t).

mean: The mean is the most common measure of average. To calculate the mean, add up all the numbers in the set of data, and then divide by the number of elements in the data.

Data set: 6, 7, 6, 8, 5, 6, 9

Number of elements in the data set: 7

$$\text{Mean} = \frac{(6 + 7 + 6 + 8 + 5 + 6 + 9)}{7} = 6.71$$

median: To calculate the median, place the data set in ascending order. The middle number is the median. If the data set has two middle numbers, then take the mean of those two middle numbers.

One middle number

Data set: 5 , 6 , 6 , 7 , 7 , 8 , 9

Median = 7

Two middle numbers

Data set: 2 , 3 , 4 , 4 , 5 , 5 , 6 , 6

Median = $\frac{(4 + 5)}{2}$ = 4.5

metric system: A system of measurement that is based on the decimal system.

Measure	Unit
Mass	gram (g), kilogram (kg), tonne (t).
Length	millimetre (mm), centimetre (cm), metre (m), kilometre (km)
Area	square centimetre (cm^2), square metre (m^2), square kilometre (km^2)
Volume	cubic centimetre (cm^3), cubic metre (m^3)
Capacity	millilitre (ml), centilitre (cl), litre (l)

A-Z Mathematics Dictionary

minuend: The number that is being subtracted from.

minuend → $20 - 4 = 16$

minus: The name given to the symbol for subtraction.

$$7 \text{ minus } 3 = 4$$
$$7 - 3 = 4$$

mirror line: (See line of symmetry.)

mixed number: A mixed number is a whole number plus a fraction. Mixed numbers can be converted in to improper fractions.

$$1\tfrac{3}{8} \Rightarrow \tfrac{11}{8}$$

mixed number   improper fraction

mode: The number that appears most often in a set of data.

Data set: 5 , 6 , 6 , 7, 7 , 7 , 8 , 9

Mode = 7

multiple: A multiple is the product of a number when it has been multiplied by another number. A quick way to remember this is that the multiples of 2 are the numbers in the 2 times table. The multiples of 3 are the numbers in the 3 times table.

Multiples of 2	Multiples of 3
2 , 4 , 6 , 8 , 10 ,………	3 , 6 , 9 , 12 , 15 ,………

multiplicand: The number that is multiplied by another number (multiplier).

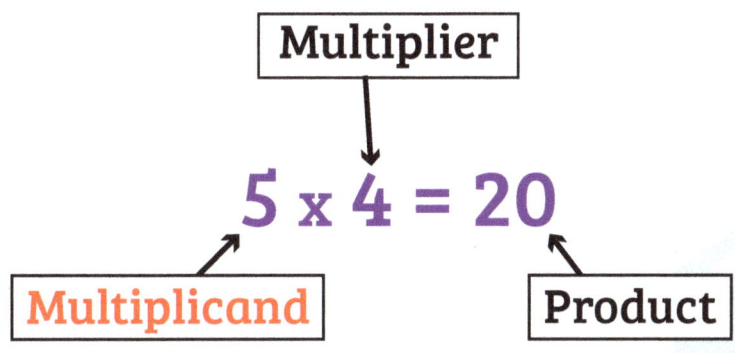

multiplier: The number that is doing the multiplying.

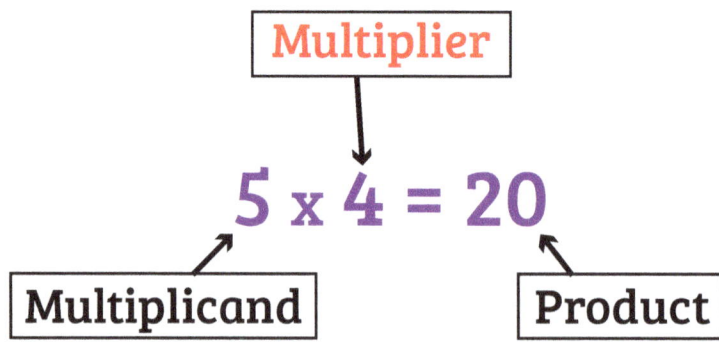

multiply: The process of adding a number to itself many times. It is a quick way to do repeated addition.

$$5 + 5 + 5 + 5 = 20 \quad \boxed{\text{Repeated addition}}$$

$$5 \times 4 = 20 \quad \boxed{\text{Multiply}}$$

negative number: A number which is less than zero.

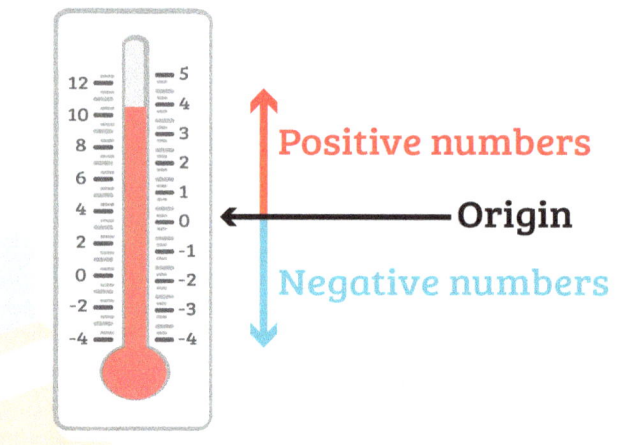

A-Z Mathematics Dictionary

net: A net is a 2-dimensional pattern of a 3-dimensional shape that has been laid flat.

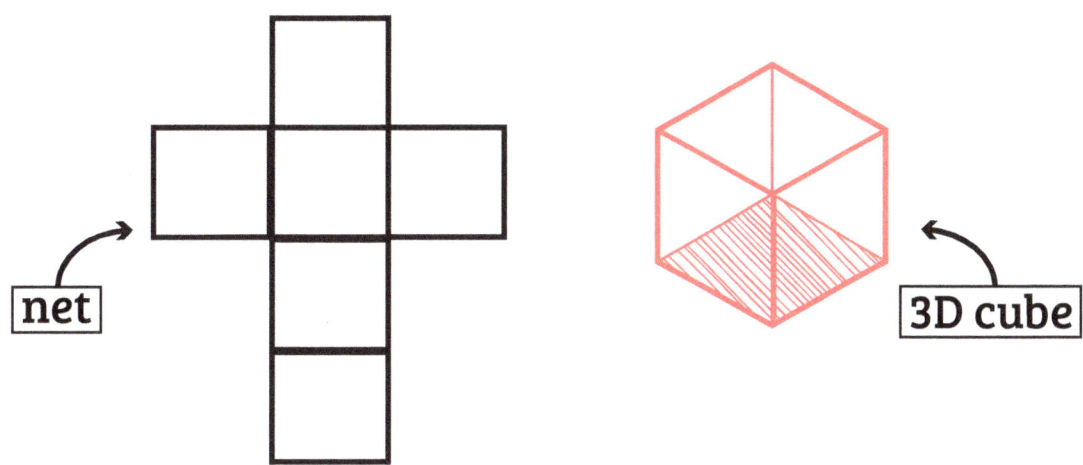

number: A number is a mathematical object used to count, measure or label and are used to show the amount of something.

number bonds: Pairs of numbers that add up to a certain number.

Number bonds to 10

10 + 0 = 10
9 + 1 = 10
8 + 2 = 10
7 + 3 = 10
6 + 4 = 10
5 + 5 = 10
4 + 6 = 10
3 + 7 = 10
2 + 8 = 10
1 + 9 = 10
0 + 10 = 10

number facts: Number facts are basic addition, subtraction, multiplication and division calculations.

number sentence: A mathematical sentence using numbers and basic symbols (+ - X ÷)

numerator: The top digit of a fraction.

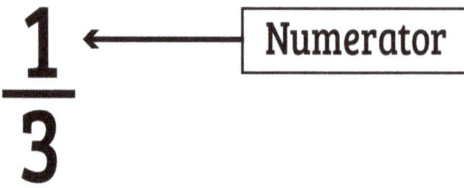

oblong: Another name for a rectangle.

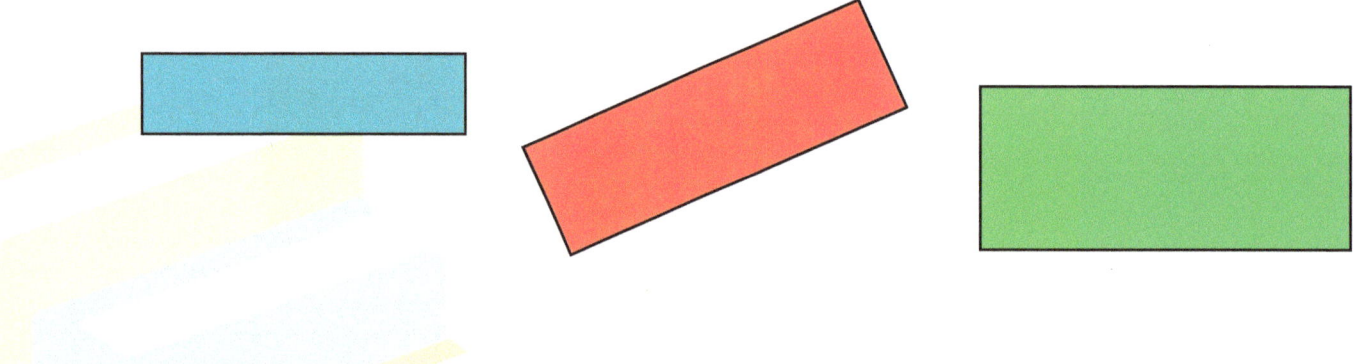

obtuse angle: An angle that is more than 90° but less than 180°.

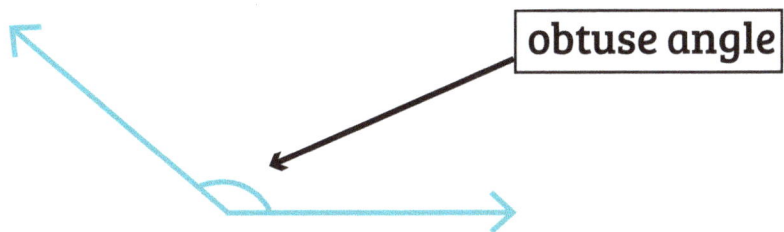

octagon: An eight-sided shape.

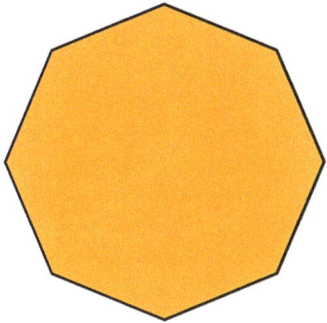

octahedron: A 3D shape (polyhedron) with eight faces. If the faces are regular the eight faces are equilateral triangles.

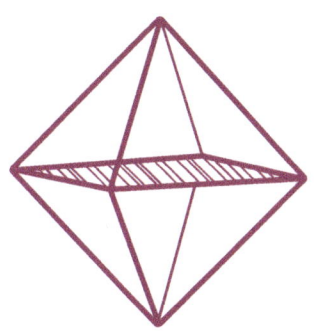

odd: A whole number that is not divisible by 2.

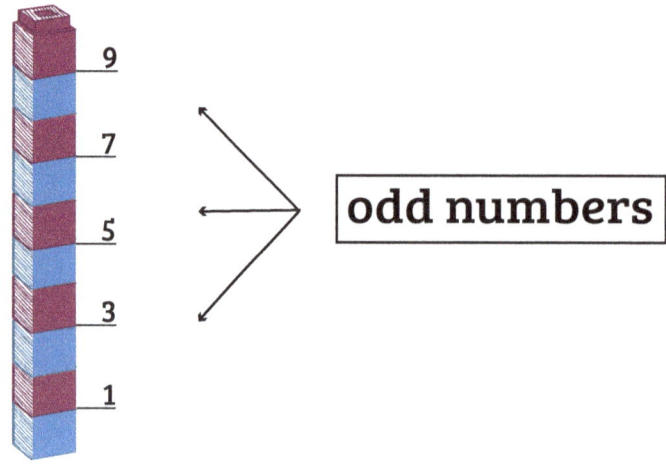

operation: A mathematical process. The most common mathematical operations are addition (+), subtraction (-), multiplication (x) and division (÷).

ordering: Placing a group of items in order of size, mass, length, thickness etc.

ordinal numbers: Tell us the position of something in a list.

origin: The point where the x and y axis meet or intersect.

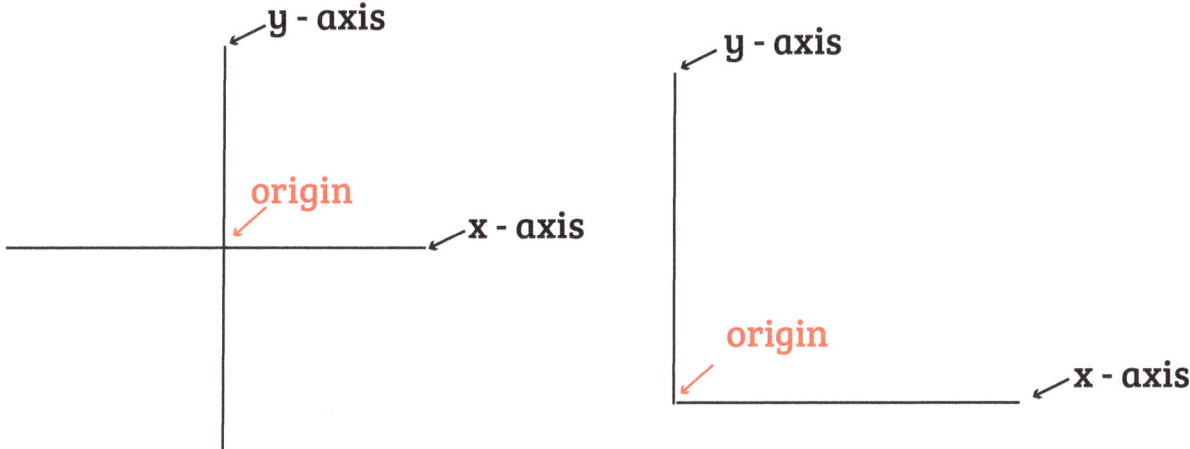

parallel: Lines travelling in the same direction, but will never meet.

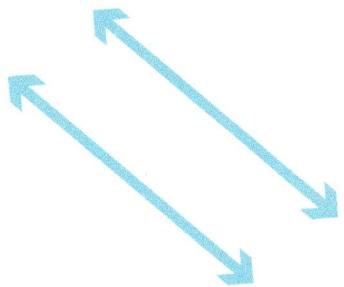

parallelogram: A four sided 2d shape where the opposite sides are equal length and parrallel.

pentagon: A five-sided, 2-dimensional shape.

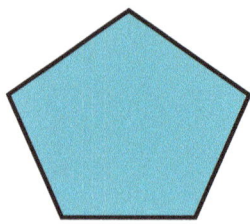

percentage: Percentage means parts per 100, or out of every 100.

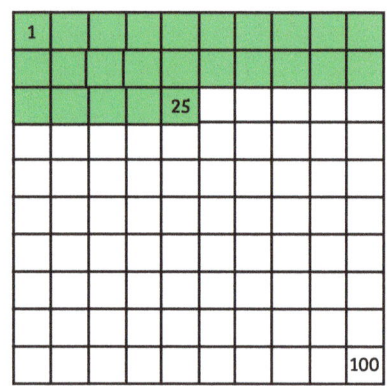

There are 25 green squares out of a total 100 squares.

25%

of the squares are green

perimeter: The total distance around a 2-dimensional shape.

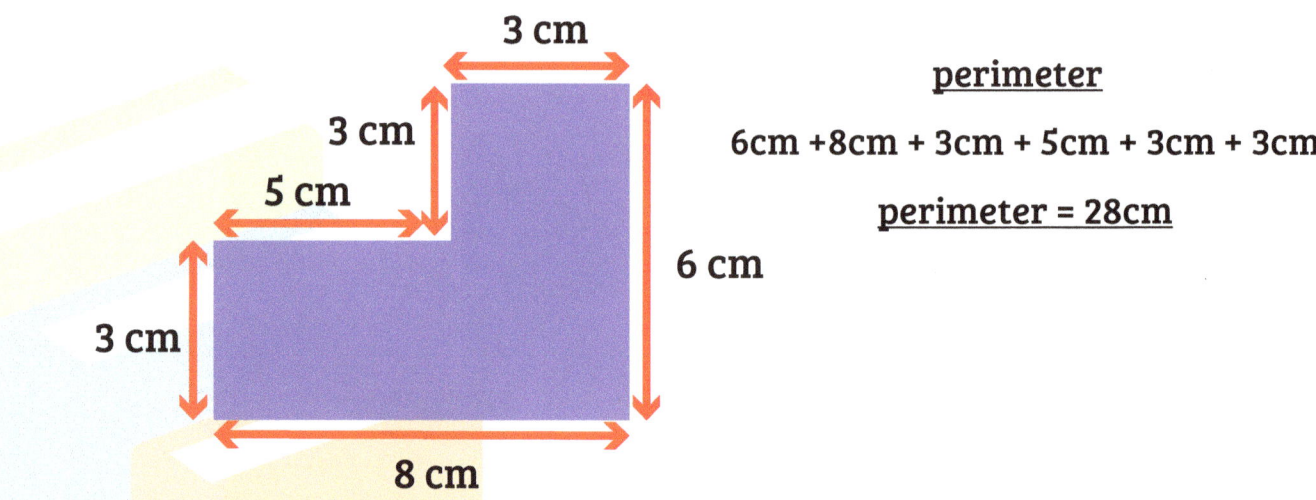

perimeter

6cm + 8cm + 3cm + 5cm + 3cm + 3cm

perimeter = 28cm

A-Z Mathematics Dictionary

perpendicular: When two lines meet at right-angles.

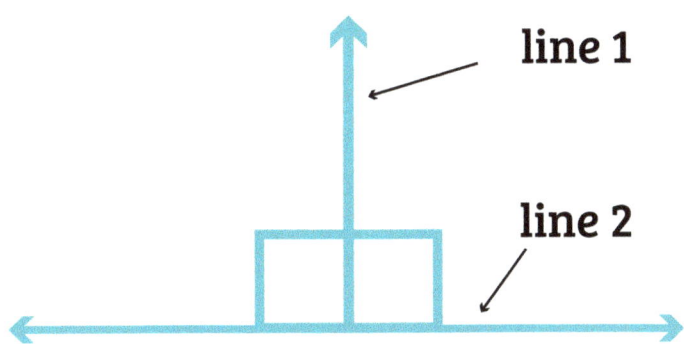

pictogram: A graph that uses pictures to represents discrete data.

pie chart: A circular graph that is cut into slices to show the data that has been collected.

Daily transport to school

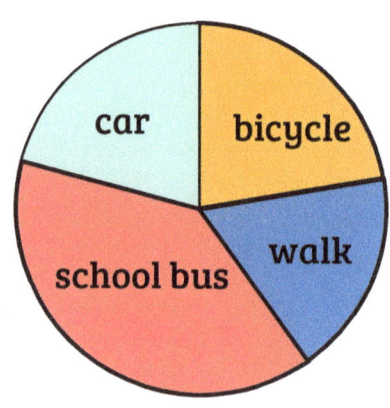

place value: The value each digit has dependent on its position.

plus: The name given to the symbol + for adding numbers together.

$$24 \text{ plus } 10 =$$

$$24 + 10 =$$

polygon: A 2-dimensional closed shape made from straight lines.

Number of sides	Name
3	Triangle
4	Quadrilateral
5	Pentagon
6	Hexagon
7	Heptagon
8	Octagon
9	Nonegon
10	Decagon
11	Hendecagon
12	Dodecagon

polyhedron: A 3-dimensional closed shape made from many flat faces. Poly means many and hedron means 'seat.' A polyhedron is a shape with many seats (faces). Example a polyhedron with 4 faces is called a tetrahedron.

Number of faces	Prefix
3	tri
4	tetra
5	penta
6	hexa
7	hepta
8	octa
9	ennea
10	deca
11	hendeca
12	dodeca

A-Z Mathematics Dictionary

positive: A positive integer is a number that is greater than zero.

i) Positive integer is a number that is bigger than zero:

$$1, 2, 3, 4, 5$$

ii) Negative integer is a number that is less than zero:

$$-1, -2, -3, -4, -5$$

prime factor: A factor of a number where the factor is also a prime number.

Factors of 20	Prime Factors of 20
1 x 20	2 and 5
2 x 10	
4 x 5	

Factors of 20 = 1, 2, 4, 5, 10 and 20

prime number: A whole number that has only two factors, 1 and itself.

Prime numbers = 2, 3, 5, 7, 11, 13, 17 ....

prism: A 3D shape that has two ends that are the same shape and these ends are joined together by rectangular or square sides.

probability: A measure of how likely it is that somthing (an event) is going to happen in the future. The probability of an event is always between 0 and 1 where 0 means it definitely won't happen and 1 means it definitely will happen.

product: The result of multiplying two numbers is the product. The product of 5 and 4 is 20.

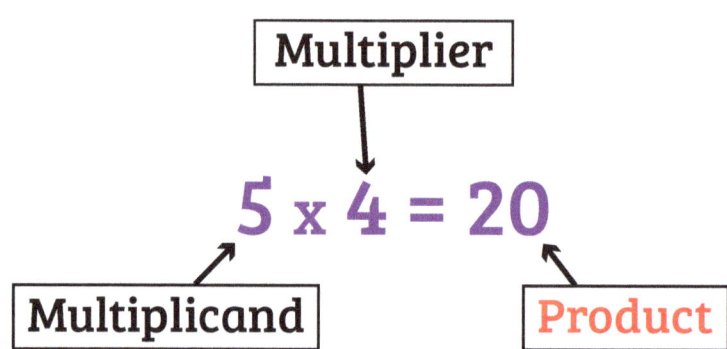

proper fraction: A fraction where the numerator is smaller than the denominator.

$$\frac{1}{3} \quad \begin{matrix} \leftarrow \text{Numerator} \\ \leftarrow \text{Denominator} \end{matrix}$$

property: A characteristic or quality something has.

properties of a square

4 right-angles
4 equal sides
opposite sides are parallel

pyramid: A 3D shape that has a polygon base and all the other faces are triangular and meet at the top.

pentagonal based pyramid

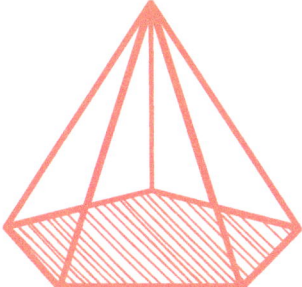

square based pyramid

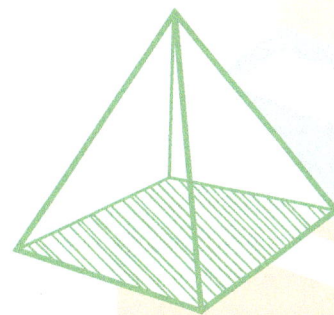

A-Z Mathematics Dictionary

quadrant: Any of the four sections created when the x and y axes cross over and intersect.

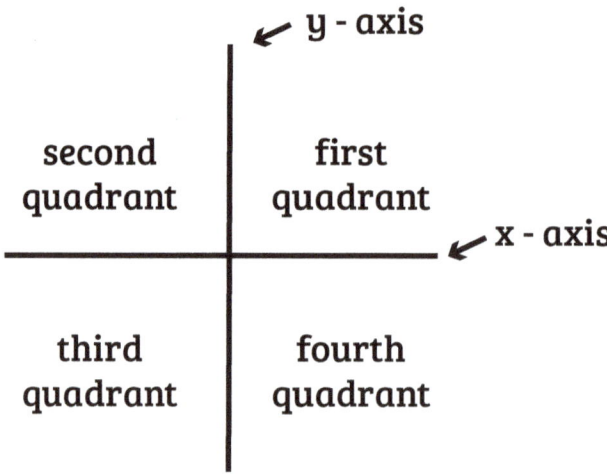

quadrilateral: A four-sided shape.

quotient: The answer when one number is divided by another number.

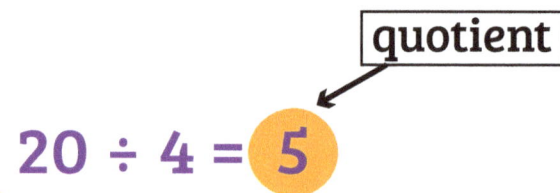

A-Z Mathematics Dictionary

radius: The distance from the centre of the circle to any point on the circumference of a circle.

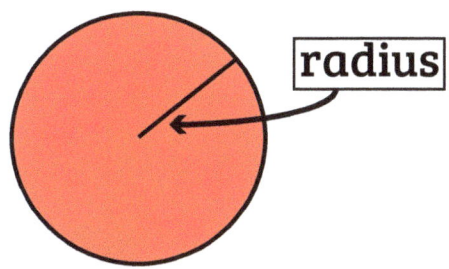

range: The difference between the largest and smallest values in a set of data.

data set: 5, 6, 6, 7, 7, 8, 9   range = 9 - 5
                                  range = 4

ratio: A ratio shows two values in relation to each other.

To make green paint, you need 3 tins of yellow paint for 1 tin of blue paint.

The ratio of yellow paint to blue paint is 3:1.

3 : 1

rectangle: (See oblong.)

reflection: An image or shape as it would be seen in a mirror.

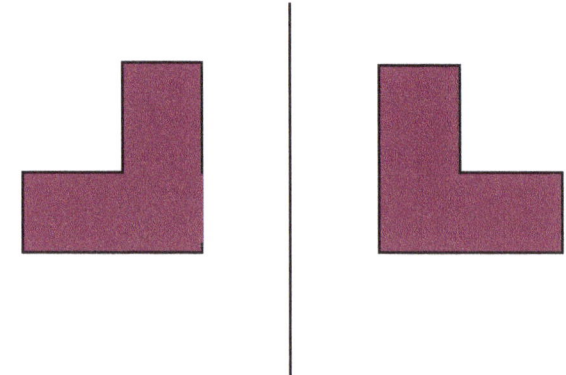

reflective symmetry: (See line of symmetry). A shape has reflective symmetry if it can be folded such that one half fits exactly on top of the other half.

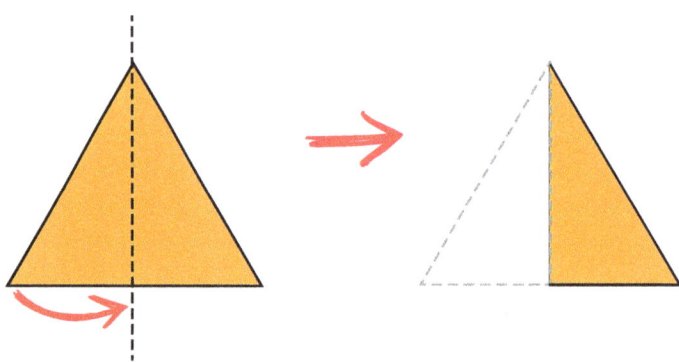

reflex angle: An angle that is more than 180⁰ and less than 360⁰.

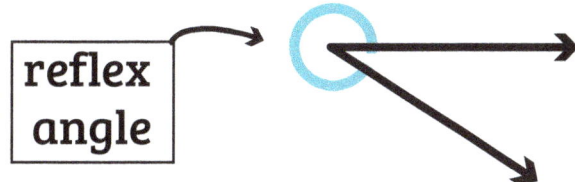

regular: A polygon where all sides are of equal length and all angles are of equal size.

rhombus: A 4-sided 2D shape whose sides are of equal length.

right angle: An angle that is exactly $90°$.

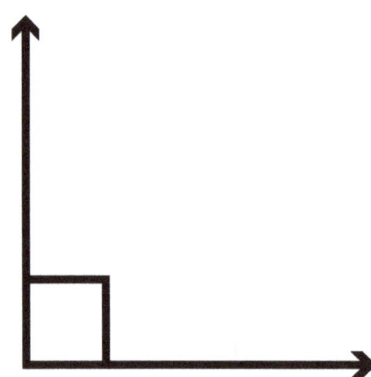

right angled: Something that contains a right angle is said to be right angled.

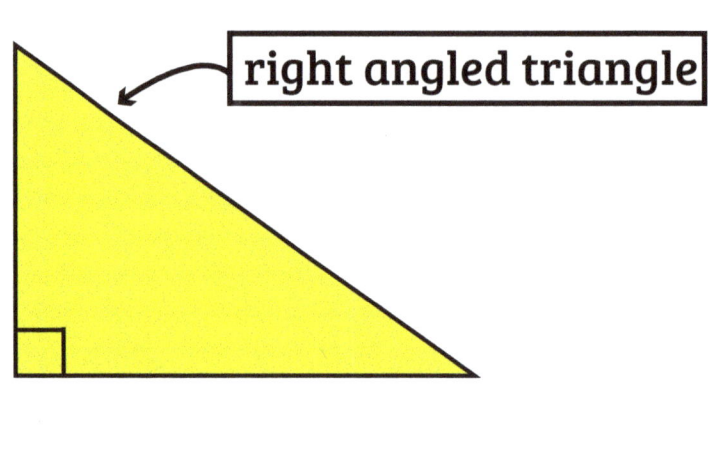

Roman numerals: The letters that the Ancient Romans used to represent numbers.

$$\begin{aligned} I &= 1 \\ V &= 5 \\ X &= 10 \\ L &= 50 \\ C &= 100 \\ D &= 500 \\ M &= 1000 \end{aligned}$$

i) When a letter is placed after another letter of equal or greater value, they are added together.

I	= 1	XI	= 11
II	= 2	XII	= 12
III	= 3	XIII	= 13
IV	= 4	XIV	= 14
V	= 5	XV	= 15
VI	= 6	XVI	= 16
VII	= 7	XVII	= 17
VIII	= 8	XVIII	= 18
IX	= 9	XIX	= 19
X	= 10	XX	= 20

ii) When a letter is placed before another letter of equal or greater value, the first letter is subtracted from the second.

$$\begin{aligned} IX &= 9 \quad (10 - 1 = 9) \\ XC &= 90 \quad (100 - 10 = 90) \\ CD &= 400 \quad (500 - 100 = 400) \end{aligned}$$

rotate: When a shape or figure turns from a fixed centre point.

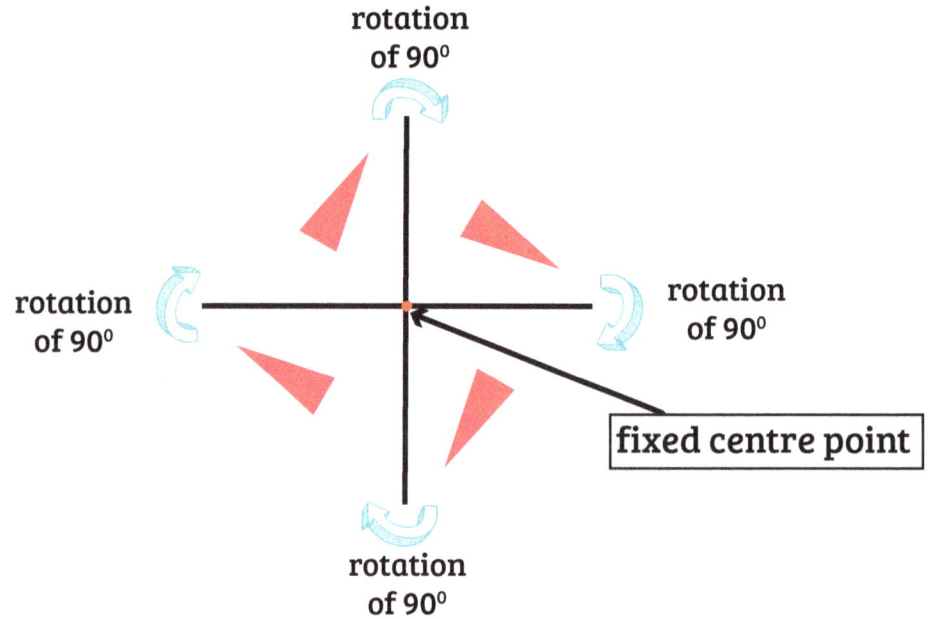

rounding: To change a number to the nearest chosen place value. Rounding helps when you want to estimate and calculate quickly.

Round 327 to the nearest hundred.

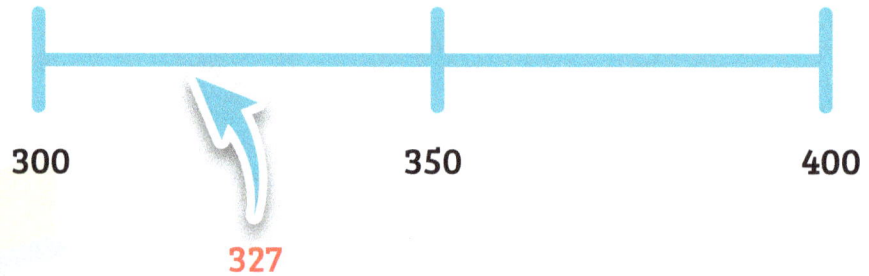

327 is closer to 300 than 400

scalene triangle: All three sides are a different length and all three angles are a different value.

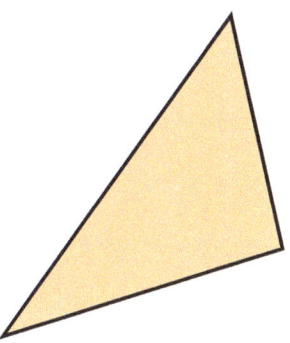

semicircle: Half a circle.

sequence: A list of numbers or objects in a specific order.

example 1:

12 , 15 , 18 , 21 , 24 , 27 , 30

example 2:

side: The straight edge of a polygon.

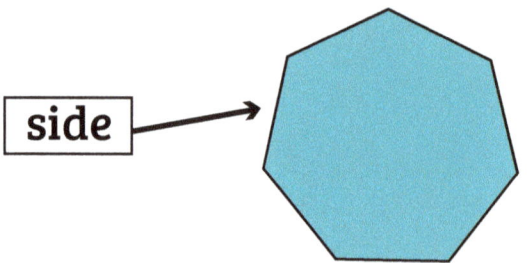

sphere: A 3D shape that is the shape of a tennis ball.

square: A regular quadrilateral. It has 4 equal sides and 4 right angles.

A-Z Mathematics Dictionary

square number: A number that is multiplied by itself. A square number can be represented in the shape of a square.

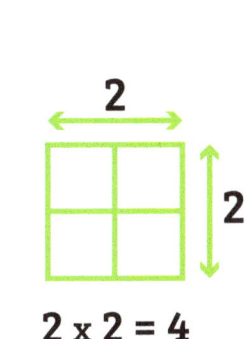
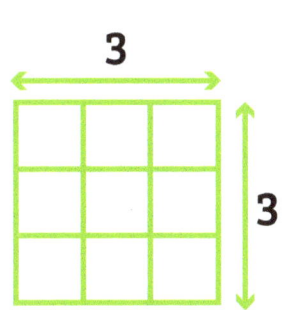
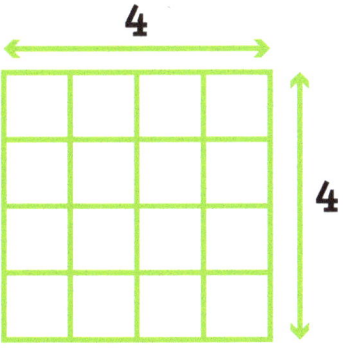

$2 \times 2 = 4$ $\qquad$ $3 \times 3 = 9$ $\qquad$ $4 \times 4 = 16$

$2^2 = 2 \times 2 =$ ④ $\qquad$ $3^2 = 3 \times 3 =$ ⑨ $\qquad$ $4^2 = 4 \times 4 =$ ⑯

square root: A square root is the name of the number that is multiplied by itself to make a square number. 2 is the square root of 4.

square number	square root
$2^2 = 2 \times 2 =$ ④	$\sqrt{4} =$ ②
$3^2 = 3 \times 3 =$ ⑨	$\sqrt{9} =$ ③
$4^2 = 4 \times 4 =$ ⑯	$\sqrt{16} =$ ④

standard form: Is a way for writing very large numbers in a short way. It saves writing many zeros.

$$10 = 10 = 10^1$$
$$100 = 10 \times 10 = 10^2$$
$$1000 = 10 \times 10 \times 10 = 10^3$$
$$10,000 = 10 \times 10 \times 10 \times 10 = 10^4$$

straight angle: An angle that is 180°.

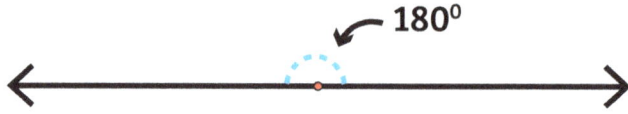

subtract: The oppposite of addition. One number (subtrahend) is taken away from another number (minuend).

A-Z Mathematics Dictionary

subtrahend: A number that is taken away from another number.

$$20 - 4 = 16$$

subtrahend → 16

sum: Another word that means add. The sum of 4 and 5 is 9. Sometimes, although incorrectly, the word sums is used to describe many different calculations.

symbol: A mark or sign that is used to represent something else.

@ = at

♻ = recycle

symmetry/symmetrical: (See line of symmetry and reflective symmetry.)

table: Information and data can be collected and placed into rows and columns whch help organise the data. These rows and columns are called a 'table'.

Transport	Tally	Total
Car	||||| |||||		11
Bus	||||| ||	7
Train	|||	3

table →

tally: A mark that is used to record things quickly. The fifth mark strikes through the previous four marks, which make it easy to count.

||||| ||||| = 10

||||| || = 7

tangram: An ancient chinese puzzle, in which a square has been divided into seven pieces (one square, one parallelogram and five triangles). The shapes can be arranged to make different designs.

A-Z Mathematics Dictionary

tessellation: A pattern made from one or more shapes that fit together perfectly.

i) Congruent shapes will tessellate together (see congruence).

ii) Some shapes will not tessellate.

iii) Some congruent shapes can be rotated to create interesting patterns.

tetrahedron: Also known as a triangular based pyramid. A tetrahedron is a 4 sided 3D shape. If it is regular, the faces are equilateral triangles. (See polyhedron.)

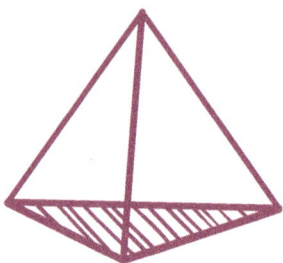

three-dimensional: (Also written as 3D or 3-D.) A solid shape that has three dimensions: height, length and depth.

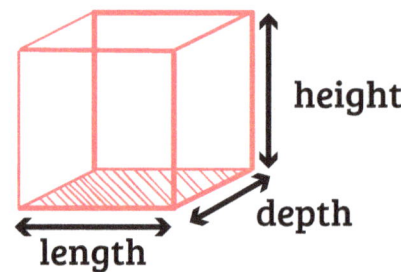

transformation: A general term used to describe four different ways a shape can be moved. Three basic transformations used in primary schools are: rotation, reflection and translation.

A-Z Mathematics Dictionary

translation: The movement of a shape over a certain distance. The shape is not changed. It is not rotated or flipped.

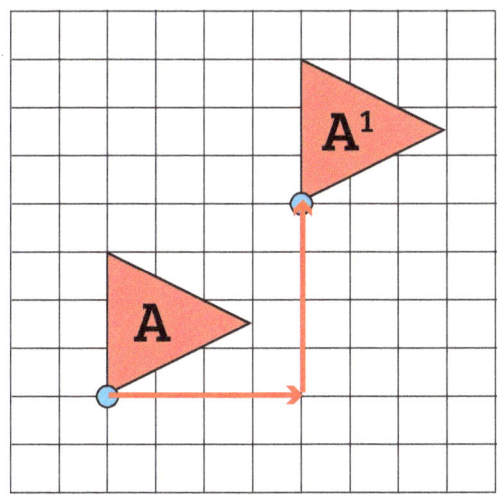

Shape A is translated 4 squares right, 4 squares up.

trapezium: A quadrilateral that has one pair of parallel sides.

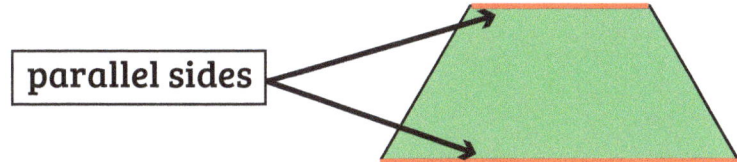

triangle: A polygon with three sides.

A-Z Mathematics Dictionary

two-dimensional: (Also written as 2D or 2-D.) A flat shape that has only two dimensions: height and length.

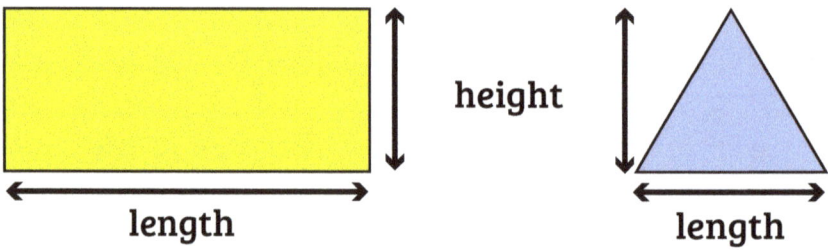

Venn diagram: A Venn diagram uses circles that overlap to show the relationship between two or more sets of data. Where the circles overlap, the data belongs to both categories that each circle represents.

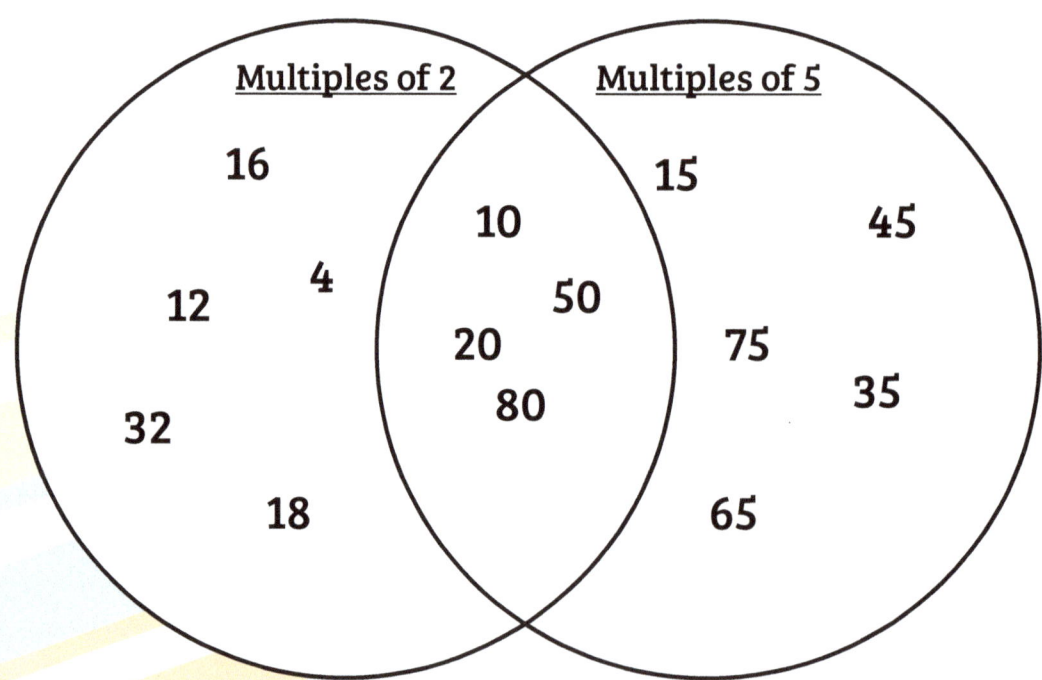

A-Z Mathematics Dictionary

vertex: (plural vertices) The point where the edges on a 3D shape meet. Often called a corner (plural corners).

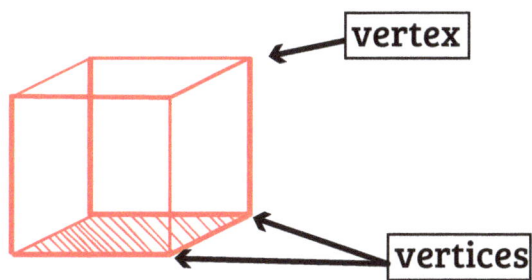

vertical: When something is at right angles or perpendicular to a horizontal plane, it is said to be vertical. Can also be described as something pointing straight up.

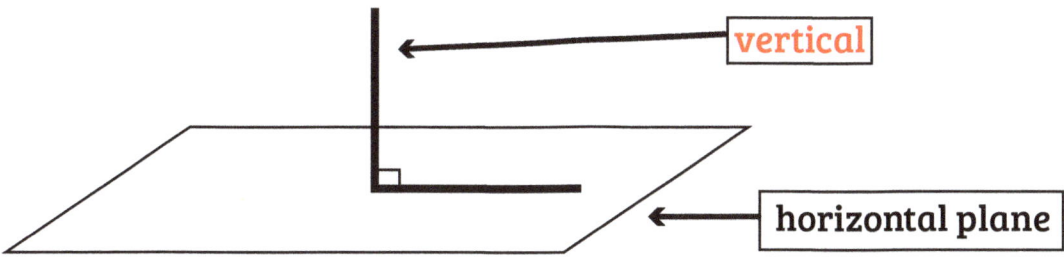

volume: The amount of space that a 3D shape can hold. The metric measurement for volume is millilitre (ml), centilitre (cl) and litre (l).

A-Z Mathematics Dictionary

weight: The force from gravity on an object. Often described as 'how heavy something is.' Weight is measured in Newtons (N) after Sir Isaac Newton. A common mistake is to say weight is measured in grams (g) which is the measurement of mass. (See mass.)

i) The mass of an object will always stay the same, but the weight of an object can change depending on the strength of gravity. A person has the same mass on Earth and on the moon, but their weight will be different as gravity is stronger on Earth.

whole numbers: Whole numbers are positve numbers that do not include decimals or fractions.

whole numbers	not whole numbers
1, 2, 3, 4, 5	5.6 , 0.04 , $5\frac{1}{2}$

x-axis: The line on a graph that runs horizontally through zero or the origin.

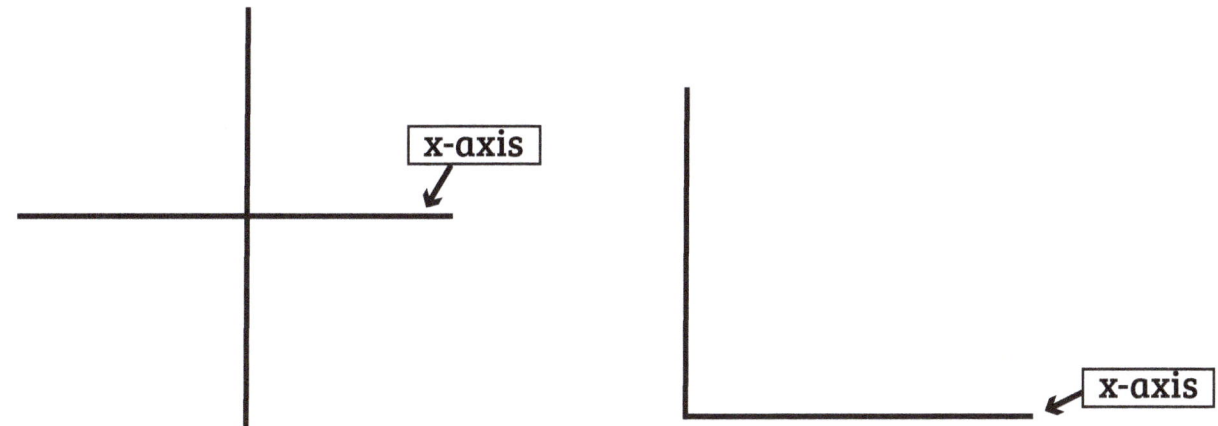

y-axis: The line on a graph that runs vertically through zero or the origin.

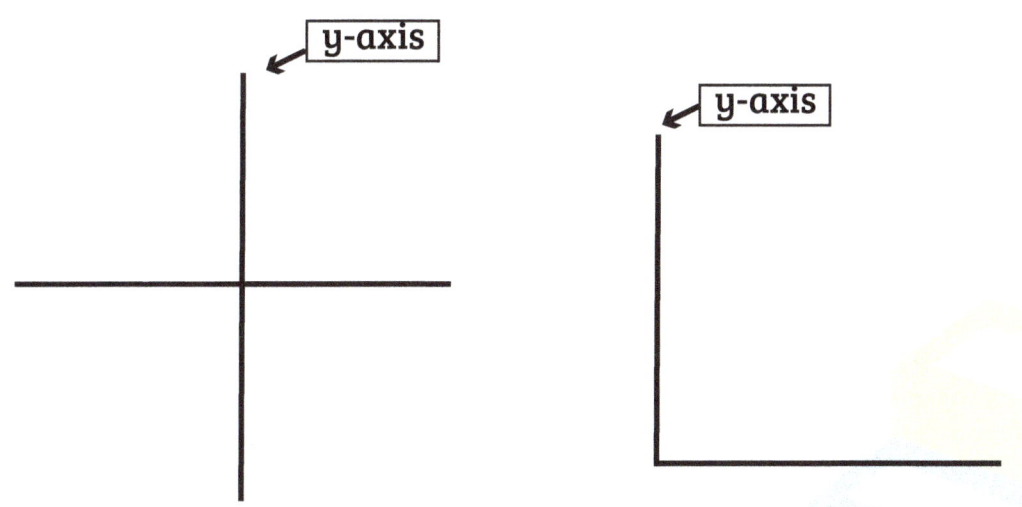